The Sweet Thief

Written by KoolCatJay

ISBN: 978-4-233-90257-7

This book is dedicated to my niece,
Ani, and nephew, Asa.
Auntie loves you very much!

Acknowledgements

Special thanks to my parents for always supporting me and my writing, especially my mom who has helped me discover that this is something I want to do for the rest of my life. Thanks, mom, and dad for everything, you're the best!
Thanks to my amazing sister, Amanda, for always listening to my excitement about my writing and encouraging me alongside Mom and Dad! Love you a bunch!
Thanks to my skills worker from Outcomes, who has been my book editor through this whole process. Thank you for every skill you have been helping me learn to be more independent and successful in my future. Thank you, you are amazing, Haley!
Thanks to the rest of the Outcomes staff who have cheered me on and supported me through this whole process. Thanks, Dave, Gretchen, Sabrina, Erin, and Dana!
Thanks to my niece, Ani, and my nephew, Asa, who listen to my stories and helped me write this story for kids their age. Without their support and their opinions, The Sweet Thief would not exist.
Many thanks to my best friend, who has also been one of my biggest fans and one of my biggest supporters. Thanks, Julz, you are the best!

Geez, Louise, do you see Cheese?

I do, I do, with his friend Bubblegum, too!

My name is Fudge,
please don't judge. My
friends know that I
never hold a grudge.

"Oh, how I'm
hungry!"

"I'm hungry, too!"

"I think I'm
in a cake kind of mood!"

Hello there, it's nice to
meet your friendly face!
My name is Peas, I say
with grace.

Yuck! Yuck! Yuck!
Oh, how I hate peas.
How could my mother name
me after something so gross
and so green?

You're all invited to a picnic, so follow me.

A picnic you say? I'm invited today! How wonderful it is for me and my friends to be joining you on a picnic today!

It's time to pack. Let's store the food
on Cheese's back!

Fudge, Bubblegum, Peas, and their dinosaur friend Cheese may be a weird combo for food, but not for these four loving goons!

As they tell stories about how they met, they look at the burgers and apples unpacked.

With their stomachs starting to rumble and tumble, they run to their food like it's their last supper.

And then the sun went away, it was now time for them to hit the hay.

Now with them all snuggled up in their beds, they have nothing to worry about with their dreams ahead.

With morning eyes, they get out of bed. Ready to tackle the day ahead.

"What should we have for breakfast?" Peas says. Both Fudge and Bubblegum say at the same time, "how about we have omelets this time?"

With their sweet tooth's, they decided to bake.

Peas wanted to bake a chocolate cake, but Fudge ached for banana cake. Bubblegum wanted to make peanut butter cookies. Then they all decided that they are sweet rookies. So with that in mind, they decided to bake any and all kinds of cookies and cakes.

As they chittered and chattered about the look of their day, they all finally decided the beach was the way.

Then out in the sun, for a good old fun day!

They decided to pack up and head home for the day.

All three friends arrived home after a
long day, to find their cupcakes and
cookies have somehow run away

And fools they were! The cookies and cupcakes were no longer whole. For all that was left was a trail full of crumbs.

Like detectives, they followed the trail. The crumbs went past Ella's home and into the mountains they roamed.

When they finally discovered the sweet thief at hand, they demanded her answer about the cupcake in her hand!

"I'm sorry", Ella said. "I meant to take one, but before I knew it I was eating them all!"

With regret behind Ella's eyes, she started to cry and cry. With sympathy behind Fudge's eyes, he says that things will be alright.

Ella learned of her mistake that you
should always ask before you take.

Ella was proud of owning her mistake. So to make up for what she did, she baked them a cake!

"We appreciate your apology," Peas, Fudge, and Bubblegum say. "And we thank you for this awesome cake!"

The End.

Hello, my author name is KoolCatJay. For my safety, my real name won't be used on any of the books I publish. As a kid and even today, I enjoy reading books.

Writing brings out a totally different side to me: it's who I am and what I love doing. So now I am pushing myself to make this a dream that I can relive my whole life.

I want young kids to pick up my book for the first time and feel the same way I do whenever I write or read someone else's stories. I want them to feel transported to a whole 'nother world that makes life fun and exciting.

My parents are encouraging me to write kid's stories, which I plan to do. I would like to try to expand my writings into poetry, books, and short stories for many different ages.